To Nate, With Love

Jenny Choi

BookLeaf Publishing

India | USA | UK

Presentation by *BookLeaf Publishing*

Web: www.bookleafpub.com

E-mail: info@bookleafpub.com

ISBN: 9789358315660

First edition 2023

PREFACE

Who knew that out there in the world- two fly ass NYC kids were living parallel lives. We met by happy accident where we both knew pretty early on - that both of us were talking and living in a language different from everyone else.

Perchance

When I first saw your face, it made me smile.
I waved at you from the across the street and I
saw you smile back bemused.
Relaxed and happy, we lightly spoke about the
future. Not yet realizing.

We spent hours on the dancefloor, singing and
laughing.
As the lights twinkled around us, I could feel
your heart beating…
It was beating as fast as mine.
I felt your hands as they slowly encircled me and
you pulled me close.
And I remember thinking how soft your lips
were.

We spoke maybe three sentences to each other
that first night, the music was so loud.
When we left, it was raining slightly as we stood
there and embraced.

That night, as I lay in bed. I smiled again
thinking about you.
I had no idea that my life was now forever
changed.

Hearts on the calendar

Our next few dates came fast and furious-
We camped out around your coffee table
With take in food & wine, the conversation
flowed for hours.

We spent hours getting to know anything and
everything about each other-
We love good music, the same artists.
We compared notes, lives, experiences.
The same experiences that you only have by
growing up in the city.

I liked how tough and gritty you could be at
times and sweet the next.
But mostly just loved looking at you and
listening to you talk.

'What an interesting person' I thought.
I could listen to him talk for hours.

And as the nights deepened, our heads bowed
together-
Our voices lower and slower as the light from
the candles flickered.

The tilt of our heads as we tried understanding each other.

In the quiet moments of those nights, I grew to understand you…
And in doing so, started falling in love before I even knew it.

Stuck on you

It's not the amazing candlelit dinners
The hours of conversation
Spending every free minute with one another

It's not the look of adoration you give me
It's not the feeling of absolute happiness you
give me
It's not the warmth you give me when you grab
my hand
It's not the way you make me blush when I catch
you staring

It's not the notifications on my phone letting me
know you're thinking of me
It's not you making plans for us

It's us together, sitting and talking earnestly
about the future
Even if we don't yet know what that looks like.
Just knowing that in some way, we will be in
each other's lives.

It's waking up in the morning knowing you're in
my life-

It's going to bed with a smile that I will see you
the next day.

It's each and every moment in between.

Lucky

His soulful eyes
His fluffy tail
His cute little walk
His heart of gold.

He pokes me with his wet nose
If it squeaks, he loves it.
He walks forward and backwards!

He wants to play when I'm working
8/10 times I give in.

He takes the biggest poops!
But he is the goodest boy ever.

And I know you two are a package deal.

Running around in my dreams

Before I met you Nate…
There was the vision of you.

A strong man.
A man with conviction and unrelenting values
Someone who does not settle
Someone who is constantly learning and
growing
Someone who despite his past and flaws he may
have

Always strives for better.

That is a courageous person.
Someone who dares to envision for more
And to dare think that they might deserve it all.

Someone who thinks the way I think.
Someone who will walk with me on this path.

I believe that someone is you.
And I think I've been looking for you for a long
time.

Because for a long time, you were just a vision
in my mind.

To make you feel my love

You stand before me as I slowly approach you
With arms open and we embrace

Your passionate kisses
And the strength of your arms around me
The candlelight illuminates your powerful body

We melt into each other.

Have I ever known passion like this before?
Have I ever kissed and loved before?

There is nothing before you.
Because now - you are all I know.

Your body, your mind, your heart, your spirit.

I can feel you with me now even when we aren't
together.
We are forever intertwined.

You are the reason

We are both two people who have loved and lost
And somewhere along the way
Had hopes and dreams that fell apart
We have memories and experiences that make us
who we are
Throughout it all - for better or worse

It is through these experiences that we try to
seek each other out
And sometimes it is through these experiences
That we misjudge the situation
Through no fault of our own

We pause, we reset, we try again.

After years of just absolute heartbreak-

Nate, you are the reason I believe in love once
again.

I won't give up

It started off with a funny feeling
Something was off
We both rubbed each other the wrong way

Before I knew it - the tears were streaming down
my face
How could I explain to you - the one person I
love so much-
How can I describe the pain that hid inside me
all this time?

The way it affects every relationship I have ever
had?
How it affects how I trust people?

No, you wouldn't understand.
No, I should turn around and just go.
But something deep in me told me I would
regret this for the rest of my life.

So I stayed.
And you held me while I sobbed.
You listened and was patient with me.

You never once gave up on me.
Your love astounds me.

Sunday kind of love

Dinners out are nice
Getting dressed up to go out for concerts is nice
Taking pictures to commemorate our special
moments are nice

But what's even nicer?

The thought of coming home to you
Cooking together on a weeknight
Watching a movie together as we try not to fall
asleep on the couch
Waking up on a Sunday as we make brunch

Backhugs
Walking Lucky together
Taking photos

I want all of these moments with you.

Will you still love me?

When the excitement of this newly sparked love
Fades to a deeper, stable love

Will you still look at me the way you do now?
Will I stare at you from across the table and
think to myself
Just how lucky I am to have this man in my life?

Will we still tell each other sweet nothings just
to see the other smile?
Will we still have the same patience as we deal
with the world and each other?

I believe in our love
I believe we never stop growing, or learning.

I love being on this journey with you.
The good, the bad - I am here for it.

For us.

So will we still love each other? In a year? In
five? In twenty?
I know there is no one else I would want to
answer that question with.

You feel like home to me

It was a busy weekend full of dinners and nights
out
You worked every single day
You never once complained and only asked what
time to pick me up?

You had fallen asleep on the way to the venue
So I turned down the music and we rode in
silence

I thought you were asleep when I heard you say
in a quiet voice

"You feel like home to me. That's how I know I
love you."

In that moment, I tried to catch my breath.
My heart had just burst into fireworks of
happiness.

Dear Nate - Letter One

It has been another wonderful month that we
have spent together.
In that time we have managed to squeeze in
music concerts, comedy shows, countless
dinners together
And more importantly - continuing to learn
about one another.

Laughing with each other as we go along.
Everytime we hang out, I can't wait until we are
together and I can see that smile again,
Kiss those lips, and never finish a movie with
you because we talk so damn much.

But I love that so much.

I hope that never stops.
I hope our curiosity about one another never
stops.

That falling deeper in love never ends.

Dear Nate - Letter One (Pt II)

It is true that we have both been in love before
That we have loved and lost.

This time however, I am not afraid of anything
with you.
And that is because I walk towards you with a
sincere heart
With earnestness to make you happy

With all that I am and that I have.

In time, all shall be revealed.
Of that, I am certain.

And I know you are worth this because you
prove to me
Everyday how amazing you are.

How thoughtful, how considerate, how smart
you are.

They say that things only come into your life
when you are ready for them.

Well, not a day goes by that I don't thank God
that you came into mine.
You're fast becoming my best friend in addition
to everything else.

I just wanted to let you know how special you
are.
And I will always try to show you just how
much.

Love, Jenny

Dearest Nate - Letter 2

I wanted to write you and tell you just how
amazing the past few months have been.
It seems we have already grown so close to one
another.

When we first met, I had this feeling I have not
experienced before
And I was a little confused.
But on the second date, it became clear.

With you - I felt safe and comfortable.
No nervousness, no anxiousness.

Only excitement and happiness.
Sheer and utter joy to spend time with you.

We could be doing anything - as long as you're
by my side, that's all that matters.

As the days go by, and we continue learning
about each other-
I am in more awe of you.

You are an amazing person, a strong man with
good family values, a spiritual person.

As person who strives to be the best and excel in every single aspect of their life.

Dearest Nate - Letter 2 (Pt II)

Motivated by your own sense of self.
How amazing is that?

I recognize that you have hard to overcome
some incredible hurdles to be where you are in
life.
I imagine those same trials have also shaped you
to be the man you are.

And in that respect I might identify with that
also.
You are a great man, Nate.
I see that and I will always try to stand by you,
supporting you in whatever endeavor you
choose to take on.

I believe in you and I am so proud of you.

I do not pretend to know what the future holds
But I know that in this short amount of time -
you have captured my heart and my soul.
And I have fallen head over heels in love with
you.

Your strength, your swagger, your humor, that
audacious laugh.

Dearest Nate - Letter 2 (Pt III)

For however long we are together-
I promise to love and cherish you.

I can't wait to see you again.
And I look forward to the future like nothing before -
Because I know it will be full of amazing days and nights together
Great laughs shared over a meal, good tunes at a concert, or staying in watching movies cozy at home.

I look forward to all that - and more with you, Nate.
You are the love of my life.

The way we communicate, the way we share and let each other in without judgement
The way we care for and respect one another is just so special.

I have never had this before.
You are my love, you are my special person.

I hope to love you forever if given the chance.

Yours,
Jenny

Picture frame

What's in a picture?
You can actually tell a lot by a picture.

The way two people are angled, their bodies
slightly facing each other
The way their heads automatically tilt together
to make a heart
The arms around each other in a warm embrace
The crinkle of the eyes as we laugh and smile in
the moment.

A picture is one moment we wish to capture for
all time.
A moment to remember, to cherish.

As your handsome face slowly takes over my
camera roll
I realize I just want more of these memories with
you.

From this moment on

My Dearest Nate,

With each passing day and moment I spend with
you-
I just know I want to spend the rest of my life
with you.

LOVE ME
GROW WITH ME.
MARRY ME.